A Gift of Flowers

Edited by Helen Exley
Photograms by Frances Berrill

≋EXLEY

Also edited by Helen Exley:
Grandmas and Grandpas (1975)
To Mum (1976)
To Dad (1976)
Happy Families (1977)
What is a Husband? (1977)
Cats (and other crazy cuddlies) (1978)
Dogs (and other funny furries) (1978)
Dear World (1978)
A Child's View of Happiness (1979)
A Child's View of Christmas (1980)
What is a Baby? (1980)
What it's like to be me (1981)
Love, a celebration (1981)
What is a Wife? (1982)
Marriage, a keepsake (1982)
For Mother, a gift of love (1983)

Published by Exley Publications Ltd,
12 Ye Corner, Chalk Hill, Watford,
Herts, United Kingdom WD1 4BS.
Selection and design © Helen Exley 1983
Photograms © Frances Berrill 1983
First published in Great Britain 1983

Printed in Great Britain by Butler & Tanner Ltd, Somerset

British Library Cataloguing in Publication Data
A Gift of flowers.
    1. Flowers — Literary collections
    I. Exley, Helen II. Berrill, Frances
    820.8'036   PR1111F/

ISBN 0-905521-64-1

One day about two years ago an old friend of mine, Eric Evans, came round
to show me a press cutting from the 'Daily Telegraph' about the work of
Frances Berrill. Frances had retired to the quaint old village of Blewbury,
on the downs in Oxfordshire, after a lifetime as a travelling puppeteer. In her
retirement she had taken to printing 'photograms' of seeds and flowers.

Instead of working with the usual camera and negatives, Frances placed
her patterns of wild things directly in the mounting of her enlarger and
produced prints directly onto light-sensitive photographic paper. No
duplicates could be made, so each print was unique.

I was collecting a countryside anthology at the time, and I took just one
look at the delicate illustrations she was creating, and rushed over to see her.
Living where she does, amidst the thatched cottages, walled gardens and
chalk streams of one of the most enchanting villages in England, it was not
hard to see where she drew the inspiration for her work. From the
flower-strewn Berkshire Downs and the profusion of her garden, she works
through the four seasons, gathering the skeletal leaves, the downy seeds and
tiny petals she needs.

We worked together over the following months, with added help from my
researcher Pam Brown, and the anthology began to take shape. My only
regret has been that some of Frances' large wall pictures have had to be so
reduced in size to fit the format of a book. They are collectors' pieces.

So my thanks go to Eric, Pam and especially Frances. Working through
the winter with her pictures has been a gift of flowers to me.

Helen Exley

The Snowdrop Minstrels

The snowdrops will soon be out, in Hampshire they are out for weeks already. But do you know the best time to see them? After dark, under a full moon.

You must look where they are, and wait. Then they seem to appear — but of course it's your eyes getting used to the dark. You see criss-cross shadows from the gnarled old apple-tree, all across the leaf-fall from last year. You see the moonlight reflected from the leaves of the laurel hedge, running down behind. And then you see them; quiet, chaste clusters, sheltering between curled couch-cushions all dead and bleached by the frost on the top; and what you thought were frost patches just beginning, or pools of moonlight, you suddenly realise are crowds, and companies, and family groups of snowdrops.

Extract from a radio talk by Norman L. Goodland

And she gave herself to all that she loved in Cossethay, passionately, because she was going away now. She wandered about to her favourite spots. There was a place where she went trespassing to find the snowdrops that grew wild. It was evening and the winter-darkened meadows were full of mystery. When she came to the woods an oak tree had been newly chopped down in the dell. Pale drops of flowers glimmered many under the hazels, and by the sharp, golden splinters of wood that were splashed about, the grey-green blades of snowdrop leaves pricked unheeding, the drooping still little flowers were without heed.

Ursula picked some lovingly, in an ecstasy. The golden chips of wood shone yellow like sunlight, the snowdrops in the twilight were like the first stars of night. And she, alone amongst them, was wildly happy to have found her way into such a glimmering dusk, to the intimate little flowers, and the splash of wood chips like sunshine over the twilight of the ground. She

4

sat down on the felled tree and remained awhile remote.

Going home, she left the purplish dark of the trees for the open lane, where the puddles shone long and jewel-like in the ruts, the land about her was darkened, and the sky a jewel overhead. Oh, how amazing it was to her! It was almost too much. She wanted to run, and sing, and cry out for very wildness and poignancy, but she could not run and sing and cry out in such a way as to cry out the deep things in her heart, so she was still, and almost sad with loneliness.

D. H. Lawrence, from 'The Rainbow'

So we went along by the hurrying brook, which fell over little cascades in its haste, never looking once at the primroses that were glimmering all along its banks. We turned aside, and climbed the hill through the woods. Velvety green sprigs of dog-mercury were scattered on the red soil. We came to the top of a slope, where the wood thinned. As I talked to Emily I became dimly aware of a whiteness over the ground. She exclaimed with surprise, and I found that I was walking, in the first shades of twilight, over clumps of snowdrops. The hazels were thin, and only here and there an oak tree uprose. All the ground was white with snowdrops, like drops of manna scattered over the red earth, on the grey-green clusters of leaves. There was a deep little dell, sharp sloping like a cup, and white sprinkling of flowers all the way down, with white flowers showing pale among the first inpouring of shadow at the bottom. The earth was red and warm, pricked with the dark, succulent green of bluebell sheaths, and embroidered with grey-green clusters of spears, and many white flowerets. High above, above the light tracery of hazel, the weird oaks tangled in the sunset. Below, in the first shadows, drooped hosts of little white flowers, so silent and sad; it seemed like a holy communion of pure wild things, numberless, frail, and folded meekly in the evening light. Other flower companies are glad; stately barbaric hordes of bluebells, merry-headed cowslip groups, even light, tossing wood anemones; but snowdrops are sad and mysterious. We have lost their meaning. They do not belong to us, who ravish them.

D. H. Lawrence, from 'The White Peacock'

5

Blossom Themes

Late in the winter came one day
When there was a whiff on the wind,
a suspicion, a cry not to be heard
    of perhaps blossoms, perhaps green
    grass and clean hills lifting roll-
    ing shoulders.
Does the nose get the cry of spring
    first of all? is the nose thankful
    and thrilled first of all?

If the blossoms come down
so they must fall on snow
because spring comes this year
before winter is gone,
then both snow and blossoms look sad;
peaches, cherries, the red summer apples,
all say it is a hard year.
The wind has its own way of picking off
the smell of peach blossoms and then
carrying that smell miles and miles.
    Women washing dishes in lonely farmhouses
    stand at the door and say, 'Something is
    happening.'
A little foam of the summer sea
    of blossoms,
    a foam finger of white leaves,
    shut these away—
    high into the summer wind runners.
Let the wind be white too.

Carl Sandburg

In the low brown woods on the lonely hill I met a pale, distracted lady all covered with pearl embroidery. Nightingales sang to each other, and never noticed that she wept, and that her tears were more beautiful than pearls. Nightingales think little of human sorrows! Do you tell me that the lady of pearls was only a blackthorn bush in bloom? If you climbed up there alone, and sat still and silent for half a day, you would know better.

Anna Lea Merritt, from 'An Artists's Garden'

. . . the White-thorn, lovely May,
Opens her many lovely eyes listening; the Rose still sleeps,
None dare to wake her; soon she bursts her crimson-curtain'd bed
And comes forth in the majesty of beauty . . .

William Blake, from 'Milton'

Loveliest of Trees, the Cherry Now

Loveliest of trees, the cherry now
Is hung with bloom along the bough,
And stands about the woodland ride
Wearing white for Eastertide.

Now, of my threescore years and ten,
Twenty will not come again,
And take from seventy springs a score,
It only leaves me fifty more.

And since to look at things in bloom
Fifty springs are little room,
About the woodlands I will go
To see the cherry hung with snow.

A. E. Housman

from Delight

Blossom — apple, pear, cherry, plum, almond blossom — in the sun. Up in the Dales when I was a child. In Picardy among the ruin of war. Afterwards at Cambridge and among the Chilterns, where I would read my publishers' manuscripts and review copies in their delicate shade. At the bottom of the canyons, at Bright Angel and Oak Creek, in Arizona. Here in our garden in the Isle of Wight. So many places, so much time; and yet after fifty years this delight in the foaming branches is unchanged. I believe that if I lived to be a thousand and were left with some glimmer of eyesight, this delight would remain. If only we could clean off the world from this Earth. But at least once every spring on a fine morning that is what we seem to do, as we stare again at the blossom and are back in Eden. We complain and complain, but we have lived and have seen the blossom — apple, pear, cherry, plum, almond blossom — in the sun; and the best among us cannot pretend they deserve — or could contrive — anything better.

J.B. Priestley

Plum-blossom

Everywhere I have sought Spring but found not Spring,
As my straw-sandals trod the cloud-capped hills.
Back again, I playfully finger and sniff the plum-blossom,
And there, at the branch-tip, is all the fullness of Spring!

Anon, Chinese

8

from The New Book of Days

How many daisies can you count on your lawn?
When you can count twelve daisies, Spring has come.

Eleanor Farjeon

Daisies

The stars are everywhere to-night,
Above, beneath me and around;
They fill the sky with powdery light
And glimmer from the night-strewn ground;
For where the folded daisies are
In every one I see a star.

And so I know that when I pass
Where no sun's shadow counts the hours
And where the sky was there is grass
And where the stars were there are flowers,
Through the long night in which I lie
Stars will be shining in my sky.

                    Andrew Young

I wandered lonely as a cloud
That floats on high o'er vales and hills,
When all at once I saw a crowd,
A host, of golden daffodils;
Beside the lake, beneath the trees,
Fluttering and dancing in the breeze.

Continuous as the stars that shine
And twinkle on the milky way,
They stretched in never-ending line
Along the margin of a bay:
Ten thousand saw I at a glance,
Tossing their heads in sprightly dance.

The waves beside them danced; but they
Out-did the sparkling waves in glee:
A poet could not but be gay
In such a jocund company:
I gazed — and gazed — but little thought
What wealth the show to me had brought:

For oft, when on my couch I lie
In vacant or in pensive mood,
They flash upon that inward eye
Which is the bliss of solitude,
And then my heart with pleasure fills,
And dances with the daffodils.

William Wordsworth

from The Grasmere Journal

*When we were in the woods beyond Gowbarrow park we saw a few daffodils
close to the water-side. We fancied that the lake had floated the seeds ashore,
and that the little colony had so sprung up. But as we went along there were
more and yet more; and at last, under the boughs of the trees, we saw that
there was a long belt of them along the shore, about the breadth of a country
turnpike road. I never saw daffodils so beautiful. They grew among the mossy
stones about and about them; some rested their heads upon these stones as on a
pillow for weariness; and the rest tossed and reeled and danced, and seemed as
if they were verily laughing with the wind, that blew upon them over the
lake; they looked so gay, every glancing, ever changing. This wind blew
directly over the lake to them. There was here and there a little knot, and a
few stragglers a few yards higher up; but they were so few as not to disturb the
simplicity, unity, and life of that one busy highway.*

Dorothy Wordsworth

from Fidelity

O *flowers they fade because they are moving swiftly; a little torrent of life*
leaps up to the summit of the stem, gleams, turns over round the bend
of the parabola of curved flight,
sinks, and is gone, like a comet curving into the invisible.

O *flowers they are all the time travelling*
like comets, and they come into our ken
for a day, for two days, and withdraw, slowly vanish again.

And we, we must take them on the wing, and let them go.
Embalmed flowers are not flowers, immortelles are not flowers;
flowers are just a motion, a swift motion, a coloured gesture;
that is their loveliness. And that is love.

D. H. Lawrence

14

from: To the Small Celandine

Pansies, lilies, kingcups, daisies,
Let them live upon their praises;
Long as there's a sun that sets,
Primroses will have their glory;
Long as there are violets,
They will have a place in story:
There's a flower that shall be mine,
'Tis the little celandine.

Eyes of some men travel far
For the finding of a star;
Up and down the heavens they go,
Men that keep a mighty rout!
I'm as great as they, I trow,
Since the day I found thee out,
Little Flower — I'll make a stir,
Like a sage astronomer.

William Wordsworth

The Lonely Flower

O Bonny is the lonesome flower
That blossoms in the lonely glen,
Self sharing dew and sun and shower,
And blooming from the eyes of men.

And bonnily awoke the morn
Upon its undefiled bloom,
The sweetest flower that e'er was born
Is hidden in the vales of broom.

Its leaves are wet with drops of dew,
And so's the woodlark's spotted breast,
Brushing them off from where she flew,
The cowslip close beside her nest.

The root increased from year to year,
Its peeps they blossomed all the May,
The school-boy knew not where to speir,
The milkmaid passed it every day.

O bonny is the lonesome flower
That blossoms in the lonely glen,
Shares by itself the sun and shower
And blossoms from the eyes of man.

John Clare

from Spring

Nothing is so beautiful as Spring —
When weeds, in wheels, shoot long and lovely and lush;
Thrush's eggs look little low heavens, and thrush
Through the echoing timber does so rinse and wring
The ear, it strikes like lightnings to hear him sing;
The glassy peartree leaves and blooms, they brush
The descending blue; that blue is all in a rush
With richness; the racing lambs too have fair their fling.
Gerard Manley Hopkins

The Throstle

'Summer is coming, summer is coming.
I know it, I know it, I know it.
Light again, leaf again, life again, love again,'
Yes, my wild little Poet.

Sing the new year in under the blue.
Last year you sang it as gladly.
'New, new, new, new'! Is it then so new
That you should carol so madly?

'Love again, song again, nest again, young again,'
Never a prophet so crazy!
And hardly a daisy as yet, little friend,
See, there is hardly a daisy.

'Here again, here, here, here, happy year'!
O warble unchidden, unbidden!
Summer is coming, is coming, my dear,
And all the winters are hidden.
Alfred Lord Tennyson

18

The First Dandelion

Simple and fresh and fair from winter's close emerging,
Forth from its sunny nook of sheltered grass—innocent,
   golden, calm as the dawn,
The spring's first dandelion shows its trustful face.
Walt Whitman

A Spring Morning

The Spring comes in with all her hues and smells,
In freshness breathing over hills and dells;
O'er woods where May her gorgeous drapery flings,
And meads washed fragrant by their laughing springs.
Fresh are new opened flowers, untouched and free
From the bold rifling of the amorous bee.
The happy time of singing birds is come,
And Love's lone pilgrimage now finds a home;
Among the mossy oaks now coos the dove,
And the hoarse crow finds softer notes for love.
The foxes play around their dens, and bark
In joy's excess, 'mid woodland shadows dark.
The flowers join lips below; the leaves above;
And every sound that meets the ear is Love.
John Clare

With tumbled hair of swarms of bees,
And flower-robes dancing in the breeze,
With sweet, unsteady lotus-glances,
Intoxicated, Spring advances.
from a Sanskrit poem

Home Thoughts from Abroad

Oh, to be in England
Now that April's there,
And whoever wakes in England
Sees, some morning, unaware,
That the lowest boughs and the brushwood sheaf
Round the elm-tree bole are in tiny leaf,
While the chaffinch sings on the orchard bough
In England — now!

And after April, when May follows,
And the whitethroat builds, and all the swallows!
Hark, where my blossomed pear-tree in the hedge
Leans to the field and scatters on the clover
Blossoms and dewdrops — at the bent spray's edge —
That's the wise thrush; he sings each song twice over,
Lest you should think he never could recapture
The first fine careless rapture!
And though the fields look rough with hoary dew
All will be gay when noontide wakes anew
The buttercups, the little children's dower
— Far brighter than this gaudy melon-flower!

                                        Robert Browning

20

Landscape as Metal and Flowers

All over America railroads ride through roses.

I should explain this is thoroughly a matter of fact.
Wherever sandy earth is piled to make a road for train tracks
The banks on either side are covered with wild, sweet
Pink rambler roses: not because roses are pretty
But because ramblers grow in cheap soil and will hold
The banks firm against rain — therefore the railroad roses.

All over America the steel-supporting flowers,
Sometimes at village depots covering the shingled station,
Sometimes embracing watertanks, but mostly endless tendrils
Out of which locomotives and pullmans flash the morning—
And tunnels the other way into whose firm, sweet evening
The whistle fades, dragging freight cars,
> *day coaches and the caboose.*

Winfield Townley Scott

Flowers

What favourite flowers are mine, I cannot say —
My fancy changes with the summer's day.
Sometimes I think, agreeing with the bees,
That my best flowers are those tall apple trees,
Who give a bee his cyder while in bloom,
And keep me waiting till their apples come.
Sometimes I think the columbine has won,
Who hangs her head and never looks the sun
Straight in the face. And now the golden rod
Beckons me over with a graceful nod;
Shaped like a sheaf of corn, her ruddy skin
Drinks the sun dry, and leaves his splendour thin.
Sometimes I think the rose must have her place —
And then the lily shakes her golden dice
Deep in a silver cup, to win or lose.
So I go on, from columbine to rose,
From marigold to flock, from flock to thrift —
Till nothing but my garden stones are left.
But when I see the dimples in her face,
All filled with tender moss in every place—
Ah, then I think, when all is said and done,
My favourite flower must be a mossy stone!

W. H. Davies

Connie went to the wood directly after lunch. It was really a lovely day, the first dandelions making suns, the first daisies so white. The hazel thicket was a lace-work, of half-open leaves, and the last dusty perpendicular of the catkins. Yellow celandines now were in crowds, flat open, pressed back in urgency, and the yellow glitter of themselves. It was the yellow, the powerful yellow of early summer. And primroses were broad, and full of pale abandon, thick-clustered primroses no longer shy. The lush, dark green of hyacinths was a sea, with buds rising like pale corn, while in the riding the

forget-me-nots were fluffing up, and columbines were unfolding their
ink-purple ruches, and there were bits of blue-bird's eggshell under a bush.
Everywhere the bud-knots and the leap of life!

               D. H. Lawrence, from 'Lady Chatterley's Lover'

If I should ever by chance grow rich
I'll buy Codham, Cockridden, and Childerditch,
Roses, Pyrgo, and Lapwater,
And let them all to my elder daughter.
The rent I shall ask of her will be only
Each year's first violets, white and lonely,
The first primroses and orchises —
She must find them before I do, that is.
But if she finds a blossom on furze
Without rent they shall all for ever be hers,
Whenever I am sufficiently rich:
Codham, Cockridden, and Childerditch,
Roses, Pyrgo and Lapwater, —
I shall give them all to my elder daughter.

                          Edward Thomas

To Daffodils

Fair daffodils, we weep to see
    You haste away so soon:
As yet the early-rising sun
    Has not attain'd his noon
      Stay, stay,
    Until the hasting day
      Has run
    But to the even-song;
And, having pray'd together, we
    Will go with you along.

We have short time to stay, as you
    We have as short a Spring;
As quick a growth to meet decay,
    As you, or any thing.
      We die,
    As your hours do, and dry
      Away,
    Like to the Summer's rain;
Or as the pearls of morning's dew
    Ne'er to be found again.

               Robert Herrick

Come-Gone

Gone the snowdrop — comes the crocus;
With the tulip blows the squill;
Jonquil white as wax between them,
And the nid-nod daffodil.

Peach, plum, cherry, pear and apple,
Rain-sweet lilac on the spray;
Come the dog-rose in the hedges —
Gone's the sweetness of the may.

Walter de la Mare

Sweet-briar fragrance on the air,
Late spring's forget-me-not, and early summer
Saxifrage and poppies, peonies and thyme,
Three young thrushes under the rhubarb leaves,
Broad beans in flower, pansies
Pricked out in boxes, too young for the border.
I have been alone; yet wish earth the better
Because of yet another summer my old eyes have seen
The beauty of this garden, the cattle grazing
Beyond the hawthorn hedge of my quiet acre.

Kathleen Raine

27

Flowering Quince

All that was rich upon a summer day,
Unnumbered, colored, brilliant and profuse,
So that we said 'the Summer's waste of flowers'
Was on that tree — a Flowering Quince it was,
And made the Lilac and the Crab-apple
Seem to withhold their blooms. And you were there,
With gifts, with graces, and with promises—
All that was rich. The Flowering Quince it was:
Unfruitfulness was all amassed in flowers.

Padraic Colum

Wistaria: Tuscan

It has come, it has come again,
This lost blue world
That I have not seen for seven years,
And now there is no other earth beside it.
O what I have missed, these seven eyeless summers,
For this is a blue world shut into itself,
This trellis of wistaria, this blue fire falling;
Its leaves drop flame to every quarter of the winds,
But I lived seven years away and came not to it,
And now the flowers are sevenfold, their honey tongues
Loll like a million bells that quiver and don't ring,
Though the air all trembles and vibrates with them.

Then, as now, their blueness was alive
With quick spangled comedies, quick turncoat rain,
That fell by the trellis and was dyed in that colour;
There was never such a heaping; such a deep piled fullness,
For the flowers lie on the pergola, like snow disastered
From some whirling cataclysm thrown and tumbled.
Let us sit in this cage of fire and think of it!
Why is no poetry so full as this,
But this is mortal with but a breath of life;
Nothing lives outside it, if you keep within,
You have seven days, and a table and a chair;
What else can you wish, you are no prisoner?
Why ever move away from here, there's nothing else?
But keep in this cage of fire and live within it,
Be the salamander in this house of flame;
Look from the windows, see the world on fire.
But now comes the aftermath, the hollow empty bathos,
For this blue flower faded at the bat-winged dusk,
It faded and went out into a lifeless nothing;
Not even did the scent stay in this worse than death.

Sacheverell Sitwell

The first week in July is the week when the regale lilies are at the peak of their perfection. Though it may sound tiresome, I cannot imagine what life would be like without the perennial enchantment of the lilies, picked from the garden, carried indoors, set in front of mirrors — (after hammering the stalks) — and gloated upon. Sniffed and savoured, preferably in solitude, examined under magnifying glasses, and, of course, set to music. If you are any sort of a pianist, if your fingers retain mobility, and if you find yourself sitting at a Steinway piano in a quiet room, confronted by a keyboard which would hold the answer to all life's problems if one could only master it, the lilies sing to you. They call the tune.

Beverley Nichols, from 'Down the Kitchen Sink'

Old Fashioned Flowers

A garden of old fashioned flowers,
Planted before grandmother was born.
The house was old then, she
Wore bonnets, long frocks,
Sat under cedar trees,
Played with solitaire and rag dolls.
The gillies now along the red wall
Make a gold spring, double daisies are
Little red cartwheels, and primroses with the strange names,
Jack-in-the-green, Hose-in-Hose, Galligaskins, and Clowns,
Speak of damp Ireland, old picture books.
And then in summer, tulips, flaked and striped,
A dream of Holland on a May morning.
And after them, roses, damask and mossed,
Scenting the English air with France and Persia,
Sulphur and shell pink, they keep close company
With dew pearls, ladybirds.
Loveliest of all, carnations and pinks,
Smelling of heady clove, sharp nutmeg;
Lining the borders of the smooth lawn,
With mignonette, fragrant verbena.
I make a posy of them all in my mind,
Remember their colours and shapes, when
The garden has only the flowers of the frost,
The smell of dead bonfires.

                              Leonard Clark

31

Cheddar Pinks

Mid the squander'd colour idling as I lay
Reading the Odyssey in my rock-garden
I espied the cluster'd tufts of Cheddar pinks
Burgeoning with promise of their scented bloom
All the modish motley of their bloom to-be
Thrust up in narrow buds on the slender stalks
Thronging springing urgent hasting (so I thought)
As if they feared to be too late for summer —
Like schoolgirls overslept waken'd by the bell
Leaping from bed to don their muslin dresses
     On a May morning.

Then felt I like to one indulging in sin
(Whereto Nature is oft a blind accomplice)
Because my aged bones so enjoyed the sun
There as I lay along idling with my thoughts
Reading an old poet while the busy world
Toil'd moil'd fuss'd and scurried worried bought and sold
Plotted stole and quarrel'd fought and God knows what.
I had forgotten Homer dallying with my thoughts
Till I fell to making these little verses
Communing with the flowers in my rock-garden
     On a May morning.

                        Robert Bridges

Bounty

The full woods overflow
    Among the meadow's gold!
A blue-bell wave has rolled,
    Where crowded cowslips grow.
The drifting hawthorn snow
    Brims over hill and wold.
The full woods overflow
    Among the meadow's gold;
The ditches are aglow!
    The marshes cannot hold
Their kingcups manifold.
    Heav'n's beauty crowds below,
The full woods overflow!

              Mary Webb

from A Midsummer Night's Dream

I know a bank whereon the wild thyme blows,
Where oxlips and the nodding violet grows
Quite over-canopied with luscious woodbine,
With sweet musk-roses, and with eglantine:
There sleeps Titania some time of the night,
Lull'd in these flowers with dances and delight . . .

              William Shakespeare

34

from The Rubaiyat of Omar Khayyam

The Rose cried: 'I am generous of largesse
And laughter. Laughingly my petals blow
Across the world; the ribbons of my purse
Snap and its load of coin flies everywhere.'

In the Garden at Night

Be still, my soul. Consider
    The flowers and the stars.
Among these sleeping fragrances,
    Sleep now your cares.
That which the universe
    Lacks room to enclose
Lives in the folded petals
    Of this dark rose.

                    Gerald Bullett

from A Treatise on Fruit Trees

. . . It is a pleasure to the eare to heare the sweet notes and tunes of singing
birds, whose company a man shall be sure to have in an orchard . . And
besides, something more this sense may receive from an Orchard by hearing the
slow motion of boughes and leeves, by soft and gentle aires, sometimes (as it
were) with a kind of singing or whistling noise, which will easily induce a
sweet and pleasant sleep in sommer time . . .

Ralph Austen

from Endymion

A thing of beauty is a joy for ever:
Its loveliness increases: it will never
Pass into nothingness; but still will keep
A bower quiet for us, and a sleep
Full of sweet dreams, and health, and quiet breathing.
Therefore on every morrow, are we wreathing
A flowery band to bind us to the earth,
Spite of despondence, of th' inhuman dearth
Of noble natures, of the gloomy days,
Of all the unhealthy and e'er-darken'd ways
Made for our searching: yes, in spite of all,
Some shape of beauty moves away the pall
From our dark spirits. Such the sun, the moon,
Trees old and young, sprouting a shady boon
For simple sheep; and such are daffodils
With the green world they live in; and clear rills
That for themselves a cooling covert make
'Gainst the hot season; the mid-forest brake,
Rich with a sprinkling of fair musk-rose blooms:
And such too is the grandeur of the dooms . . .

John Keats

An aster, a farewell-summer flower, stays long in the last fall weeks,
Lingers in fence corners where others have shivered and departed.
The whites have mentioned it as the last-rose-of-summer, the red man saying,
    'It-brings-the-frost.'
Late in the morning and only when sun-warmed does the flower-of-an-hour,
    the good-night-at-noon, open a while and then close its blossoms.
Even in the noon sun the scarlet pimpernel may shut its petals, as a storm
    sign, earning its ancient name of wink-a-peep and sometimes called the
    poor-man's-weather-glass.
John-go-to-bed-at-noon is the goat's beard plant shutting itself at twelve
    o'clock and showing again only when the next day's sun is out.
One looped vine of the hop-growers is a kiss-me-quick and more than one red
    flower blooming in rock corners is a love-lies-bleeding or a
    look-up-and-kiss-me.

The saskatoon is a shadblow looming white in the spring weeks when the shad
    are up the rivers and spawning,
And hanging its branches with the June berry, the Indian cherry, it is still
    the saskatoon fed by the melted snows of chinooks.

The toadflax, the ox-eye daisy, the pussy willow, rabbit bells, buffalo clover,
   swamp candles and wafer ash,
These with the windrose and the rockrose, lady slippers, loose-strife,
   thorn-apples, dragon's blood, old man's flannel,
And the horse gentian, dog laurel, cat-tails, snakeroot, spiderwort, pig
   weed, sow thistle, skunk cabbage, goose grass, moonseed, poison hemlock,
These with the names on names between horse radish and the
   autumn-flowering orchid of a lavish harvest moon —
These are a few of the names clocked and pronounced by the people in the
   moving of the earth from season to season.

The red and white men traded plants and words back and forth.
The Shawnee haw and the Choctaw root, the paw paw, the potato, the
   cohosh and your choice of the yellow puccoon or white,
A cork elm or a western buckthorn or a burning bush, each a wahoo and all
   of the wahoo family
These from the tongues of name givers, from a restless name changer, the
   people.

Carl Sandburg

Exile

Then, I had no doubt
That snowdrops, violets, all creatures, I myself
Were lovely, were loved, were love.
Look, they said,
And I had only to look deep into the heart,
Dark, deep into the violet, and there read,
Before I knew of any word for flower or love,
The flower, the love, the word.

They never wearied of telling their being; and I
Asked of the rose, only more rose, the violet
More violet; untouched by time
No flower withered or flame died,
But poised in its own eternity, until the looker moved
On to another flower, opening its entity.

I see them now across a void
Wider and deeper than time and space.
All that I have come to be
Lies between my heart and the rose,
The flame, the bird, the blade of grass.
The flowers are veiled;
And in a shadow-world, appearances
Pass across a great 'toile vide'
Where the image flickers, vanishes,
Where nothing is, but only seems.
But still the mind, curious to pursue
Long followed them, as they withdrew
Deep within their inner distances,
Pulled the petals from flowers, the wings from flies,
Hunted the heart with a dissecting-knife
And scattered under a lens the dust of life;
But the remoter, stranger

Scales iridescent, cells, spindles, chromosomes,
Still merely are:
With hail, snow-crystals, mountains, stars,
Fox in the dusk, lightning, gnats in the evening air
They share the natural mystery,
Proclaim I AM, and remain nameless.

Sometimes from far away
They sign to me;
A violet smiles from the dim verge of darkness
A raindrop hangs beckoning on the eaves,
And once, in long wet grass,
A young bird looked at me.
Their being is lovely, is love;
And if my love could cross the desert self
That lies between all that I am and all that is,
They would forgive and bless.

Kathleen Raine

from The Testament of Beauty

Or as I well remember one highday in June
bright on the seaward South-downs, where I had come afar
on a wild garden planted years agone, and fenced
thickly within live-beechen walls: the season it was
of prodigal gay blossom, and man's skill had made
a fair-order'd husbandry of that native pleasaunce:
But had there been no more than earth's wild loveliness,
the blue sky and the soft air and the unknown flowersprent lawns,
I would have lain me down and long'd, as then I did,
to lie there ever indolently undisturb'd, and watch
the common flowers that starr'd the fine grass of the wold,
waving in gay display their gold-heads to the sun,
each telling of its own inconscient happiness,
each type a faultless essence of God's will, such gems
as magic master-minds in painting or music
threw aside once for man's regard or disregard;
things supreme in themselves, eternal, unnumber'd
in the unexplored necessities of Life and Love.

Robert Bridges

Rag-wort

Nobody considers rag-wort a flower.
It comes too late, and in wrong places.
Some say it stinks of rotten apples
And sours the ground it grows upon.
But I have watched for many an hour
The pattern a colony of it traces
Along a river's bank, the sun
Spilled over it and gilding the ripples
When no other colour can be seen
But green, mile after mile of green.

In the minority, I'll concede
To those who hold it in disdain,
That rag-wort is a rebel weed
And should be rooted out, or ploughed
Under, never to be seen again.
But still, in memory, a cloud
Of meadow butterflies will hover
Where that untidy blossom shook
Gold-dust into the passing brook.
Only those ephemeral wings
Will grieve; and perhaps one who sings.

                    Richard Church

from: Of Gardens

And because the breath of flowers is far sweeter in the air (where it comes and goes, like the warbling of music) than in the hand, therefore nothing is more fit for that delight, than to know what be the flowers and plants that do best perfume the air. Roses, damask and red, are fast flowers of their smells; so that you may walk by a whole row of them, and find nothing of their sweetness; yea, though it be in a morning's dew. Bays, likewise, yield no smell as they grow; rosemary little, nor sweet marjoram; that which, above all others, yields the sweetest smell in the air is the violet, specially the white double violet, which comes twice a year, about the middle of April, and about Bartholomew-tide. Next to that is the musk-rose; then the strawberry leaves dying with a most excellent cordial smell; then the flowers of the vines

— it is a little dust, like the dust of a bent, which grown upon the cluster in the first coming forth. Then sweet briar; then wallflowers, which are very delightful to set under a parlour or lower chamber window; then pinks and gilliflowers, specially the matted pink, and clove gilliflower; then the flowers of the lime tree; then the honeysuckles, so they be somewhat afar off. Of bean flowers I speak not, because they are field flowers; but those which perfume the air most delightfully, not passed by as the rest, but being trodden upon and crushed are three — that is burnet, wild thyme, and water mints; therefore you are to set whole alleys of them, to have the pleasure, when you walk or tread.

Francis Bacon

The Dandelion

I am the sun's remembrancer, the boy
Who runs in hedgerow, and in field and garden,
Showing his badge, a round-faced golden joy
With tips of flame. I bear my master's pardon
For my long, greedy roots. I bring his message
And pay his sovereign coin for my passage.
If any call me robber of the soil,
Let him but wait on windy weather, note
How easily, without a mortal's toil,
I change my gold to silver treasure, float
The fairy mintage on the air, and then
Defy the curse of all industrious men.

                              Richard Church

Wildflowers

You gave me dandelions.
They took our lawn
by squatters' rights—
round suns rising
in April, soft moons
blowing away in June.
You gave me lady slippers,
bloodroot, milkweed,
trillium whose secret number
the children you gave me
tell. In the hierarchy
of flowers, the wild
rise on their stems
for naming.
Call them weeds.
I pick them as I
picked you,
for their fierce,
unruly joy.

          Linda Pastan

Hurrahing in Harvest

Summer ends now; now, barbarous in beauty, the stooks rise
Around; up above, what wind-walks! what lovely behaviour
Of silk-sack clouds! has wilder, wilful-wavier
Meal-drift moulded ever and melted across skies?

I walk, I lift up, I lift up heart, eyes,
Down all that glory in the heavens to glean our Saviour;
And, eyes, heart, what looks, what lips yet gave you a
Rapturous love's greeting of realer, of rounder replies?

And the azurous hung hills are his world-wielding shoulder
Majestic — as a stallion stalwart, very-violet-sweet! —
These things, these things were here and but the beholder
Wanting; which two when they once meet,
The heart rears wings bold and bolder
And hurls for him, O half hurls earth for him off under his feet.

Gerard Manley Hopkins

The Lone Swallows

I was alone with the wheat that I loved. Moving over the field my feet were drenched in an instant by the dew. Lying at full length on the earth, I pressed my face among the sweet wistfulness of stalks, stained and glowing as with some lambent fire, pale, mysterious. On each pale flame-blade depended a small white light, a dew-drop in which the light of the moon was imprisoned. Each flag of wheat held the beauty of pure water, and within the sappy blades glowed the spirit of the earth — in the spectral silence a voice spoke of its ancient lineage: of the slow horses that had strained to the wooden plough through the ages, scarring the glebe in long furrows that must be sown with corn; race after race of slow horses moving in jangling harness to the deep shouts of the heavy men. Generation after generation of men, bent with age and unceasing labour, plodding the earth, sowing the yellow grains that would produce a million million berries for mankind.

Henry Williamson

Approach of Autumn

The early violets we saw together,
Lifting their delicate swift heads
As if to dip them in the water, now wither,
Arching no more like thoroughbreds.

Slender and pale, they flee the rime
Of death: the ghosts of violets
Are running in a dream. Heart-flowering time
Decays, green goes, and the eye forgets.

Forgets? But what spring-blooded stock
Sprouts deathless violets in the skull
That, pawing on the hard and bitter rock
Of reason, make thinking beautiful?

                              Stanley Kunitz

from To Autumn

Season of mists and mellow fruitfulness,
    Close bosom-friend of the maturing sun;
Conspiring with him how to load and bless
    With fruit the vines that round the thatch-eves run;
To bend with apples the moss'd cottage-trees,
    And fill all fruit with ripeness to the core;
        To swell the gourd, and plump the hazel shells
    With a sweet kernel; to set budding more,
And still more, later flowers for the bees,
Until they think warm days will never cease,
    For Summer has o'er-brimm'd their clammy cells.

Where are the songs of Spring? Ay, where are they?
    Think not of them, thou hast thy music too, —
While barred clouds bloom the soft-dying day,
    And touch the stubble-plains with rosy hue;
Then in a wailful choir the small gnats mourn
    Among the river sallows, borne aloft
        Or sinking as the light wind lives or dies;
And full-grown lambs loud bleat from hilly bourn;
    Hedge-crickets sing; and now with treble soft
    The red-breast whistles from a garden-croft;
        And gathering swallows twitter in the skies.

                    John Keats

To Chrysanthemums

Late comers! Ye, when autumn's wealth is past;
　　When pale October strips the yellowing leaves;
　　When on our garden lawns and dripping eaves
　　The rain-soaked foliage of the elm is cast.
When 'neath grey skies the wild Atlantic blast
　　Searches the flowerbed for each bloom that cleaves
　　To blackening tendrils; when November weaves
　　Fretwork of frost, and winter frowns at last;
Ye in the year's decay and death of hope
　　Dawn with your hues auroral, hues of rose,
　　Saffron and ivory, amber, amethyst;
More delicate, more dear, more true than those
　　Gay blossoms which the July sunbeams kissed,
　　Purer of scent than honey heliotrope.

　　　　　　　　　　　John Addington Symonds

Christmas Rose

Midwinter, and the dead earth
Suddenly parts to give birth
To thick clusters of stiff flowers
Whiter than scattered pear tree showers,
Marble monuments or morning milk,
Smoother than pebbles or old silk,
I touch each blossom, where they lie
With polished leaves and golden eye,
The hellebore of the January snows,
The plant I call the Christmas rose.

Leonard Clark

ACKNOWLEDGEMENTS: *The publishers gratefully acknowledge permission to reproduce copyright material. Every effort has been made to trace copyright holders, but in a few cases this has proved impossible. The publishers would be interested to hear from any copyright holders not here acknowledged.* GERALD BULLETT, 'Be still, my soul. Consider'. *Reprinted from* Poems *published by Cambridge University Press. Reprinted by permission of Mrs Rosemary Seymour;* RICHARD CHURCH, 'Rag-wort' *from* The Inheritors (Heinemann) *and* 'The Dandelion' *from* Collected Poems. *Reprinted by permission of Laurence Pollinger Ltd and the Estate of Richard Church;* LEONARD CLARK, 'Christmas Rose', *from* Collected Poems and Verses for Children *and* 'Old Fashioned Flowers' *from* Four Seasons. *Reprinted by permission of Dobson Books Ltd;* PADRAIC COLUM, 'Flowering Quince', *from* The Vegetable Kingdom. *Copyright © 1954, renewed 1982 by Padraic Colum. Reprinted by permission of Indiana University Press;* W. H. DAVIES, 'Flowers' *from* Complete Poems. *Reprinted by permission of Jonathan Cape, The Executors of the W. H. Davies Estate and Wesleyan University Press;* WALTER DE LA MARE, 'Come — Gone'. *Reprinted by permission of the Literary Trustees of Walter de la Mare and The Society of Authors as their representative;* ELEANOR FARJEON, *Extract from* The New Book of Days *published by Oxford University Press;* NORMAN GOODLAND, *Extract from* 'The Snowdrop Minstrels' *from* Woman's Hour: A third selection *published by BBC. Reprinted by permission of the author;* A. E. HOUSMAN, 'Loveliest of trees, the cherry now', *from* Collected Poems *published by Jonathan Cape Ltd. (UK) and Holt Rinehart & Winston, Inc (U.S.A.). Reprinted by permission of The Society of Authors as the literary representative of the Estate of A. E. Housman, and the publishers;* STANLEY KUNITZ, 'Approach of Autumn' *from* The Poems of Stanley Kunitz 1928-1978. *Copyright © 1930 Stanley Kunitz. Reprinted by permission of Little, Brown & Co., in association with the Atlantic Monthly Press;* D. H. LAWRENCE, *Extracts from* Lady Chatterley's Lover *and* The White Peacock. *Reprinted by permission of Laurence Pollinger Ltd and the Estate of Frieda Lawrence Ravagli. Verses 2, 3 and 4 from* 'Fidelity' *from* The Complete Poems of D. H. Lawrence, *collected and edited by Vivian de Sola Pinto and F. Warren Roberts. Copyright 1964, 1971 by Angelo Ravagli and C. M. Weekley, executors of the Estate of Frieda Lawrence Ravagli, published by William Heinemann. Reprinted by permission of Viking Penguin, Inc, Laurence Pollinger and the Estate of Frieda Lawrence Ravagli. Extract from* The Rainbow, *copyright 1915 by D. H. Lawrence copyright renewed 1943 by Frieda Lawrence Ravagli. Reprinted by permission of Viking Penguin Inc, Laurence Pollinger and the Estate of Frieda Lawrence Ravagli;* ANNA LEA MERRITT, *Extract from* An Artist's Garden *published by George Allen & Unwin. Reprinted by permission of the publishers;* BEVERLEY NICHOLS, *Extract from* Down the Kitchen Sink, *published by W. H. Allen. Reprinted by permission of the publishers;* LINDA PASTAN, 'Wildflowers' *from* Selected Poems *published by John Murray (Publishers) Ltd and from* P.M.-A.M. New and Selected Poems *published by W. W. Norton & Co. Inc., Reprinted by permission of the publishers, Copyright © 1982 by Linda Pastan;* J. B. PRIESTLEY, *Extract from* Delight *published by William Heinemann Ltd. Reprinted by permission of the publisher and Little, Brown and Company;* THE RUBAIYYAT OF OMAR KHAYAM. *Extract from* The Rubaiyyat of Omar Khayam *published by Penguin Books Ltd. Reprinted by permission of Robert Graves and Omar Ali-Shar;* KATHLEEN RAINE, 'Sweet-briar fragrance on the air' *and* Exile *from* Collected Poems, *published by George Allen & Unwin. Reprinted by permission of the publishers;* CARL SANDBURG, 'An aster . . .' *and* 'Blossom Themes' *from* Good Morning America. *Copyright 1928, 1956 by Carl Sandburg. Reprinted by permission of Harcourt Brace Jovanovich, Inc.;* SANSKRIT, *Extract from* Poems from the Sanskrit, *translated by John Brough. Penguin Books Ltd. Copyright © John Brough 1968. Reprinted by permission of the publishers;* SACHEVERELL SITWELL, *Extract from* Wistaria: Tuscan *published by Macmillan. Reprinted by permission of David Higham Associates;* WINFIELD TOWNLEY SCOTT, 'Landscape as Metal and Flowers' *from* Collected Poems 1937-1962. *Reprinted by permission of Macmillan Publishing Co. Copyright © 1941, 1962 by Winfield Townley Scott;* WILLIAM CARLOS WILLIAMS, 'Primrose' *from* Collected Earlier Poems. *Copyright © 1938 by New Directions Publishing Corporation. Reprinted by permission of New Directions;* HENRY WILLIAMSON, *Extract from* The Lone Swallows. *Reprinted by permission of The Henry Williamson Literary Estate;* MARY WEBB, 'Bounty' *from* 51 Poems, *Jonathan Cape. Reprinted by permission of the publishers and the Executors of the Estate of Mary Webb;* ANDREW YOUNG, 'Daisies' *from* Complete Poems *published by Martin Secker & Warburg. Reprinted by permission of the publishers.*

Other gift books from Exley Publications

Love, a celebration, £4.95. *Writers and poets old and new have captured the feeling of being in love in this very personal collection. Some of the best love messages of all ages are sensitively illustrated with fine photograms and grey screened photographs. And to enhance the collection the book is bound in a rich wine-red suedel cloth and finished with gold tooling, gift wrapped and sealed with wax. This is our best-selling book — it makes an ideal love-gift.*

Marriage, a keepsake, £4.95. *In the same series, but with a dove-grey suedel cover. This collection of poems and prose celebrates marriage with some of the finest love messages between husbands and wives. A gift for all ages — from those about to be married to those who have known fifty good years and more together. Giftwrapped with sealing wax.*

For Mother, a gift of love, £4.95. *The third collection in the series is bound in pale blue suedel, finished with gold blocking and gift-wrapped. Varied sources, from Ogden Nash to Noël Coward, from C. Day Lewis to D. H. Lawrence, from Margaret Mead to Rudyard Kipling pay tribute to their own mothers. The book is illustrated throughout with grey screened photos and paintings by people like Van Gogh and Picasso.*

Ziggy: Plants are some of my favourite people, £2.95. *This is a popular book of Ziggy cartoons about the born loser whose endearing failures make him appeal to all ages. Ziggy and his plant have a very special relationship. His plant reacts emotionally, complains a great deal, gets depressed a lot, is jealous of the attention Ziggy gives any of his annuals and hates being left alone. A must for anyone who is potty about plants — or about Ziggy.*

Sharing Nature with Children, £3.50. *A quiet, beautiful book for parents and teachers who want their children to grow up with a love of nature. Forty-one games, which can be played in the garden as well as the countryside, bring children close to living things.*

Is There Life After Housework?, £4.95. *This revolutionary book shows how you can save up to 75% of the time you now spend on cleaning. The author Don Aslett heads one of the largest cleaning firms in the world and he shows how professional methods — the right equipment, the right cleaning liquids, and a ruthless attitude to clobber and junk, can really work in the home. Illustrated throughout with lively cartoons.*

Grandmas and Grandpas, £3.95. *Children are close to grandparents, and this book of children's sayings reflects that warmth: "Your granny loves you, no matter what you do"; "A grandma is old on the outside but young on the inside"; "A granny is jolly and when she laughs a warmness spreads over you." This is a very, very popular book, which makes a particularly loving present for grandparents.*

To Dad, £3.95. *'Fathers are always right, and even if they're not right, they're never actually wrong'. Dads will love this book — it's so true to life! A regular favourite.*

To Mum, £3.95. *'When I'm sad she patches me up with laughter.' A thoughtful, joyous gift for Mum, entirely created by children. Get it for Mother's Day or her birthday.*

Give Happiness a Chance, £4.95. *Quiet, beautiful and sensitive. This book has swept Europe, with sales of one and a half million copies. A memorable and thoughtful gift, especially valued, perhaps, by someone who is lonely.*

Simply order through your bookshop, or by post from Exley Publications Ltd., Dept GF, 12 Ye Corner, Chalk Hill, Watford, Herts WD1 4BS. Please add 15p in the £ as a contribution to postage and packing.